APR 2019

BEHIND THE CURTAIN
Act Out History's BIGGEST Dramas

UNION TRIUMPH

BATTLE OF GETTYSBURG

Virginia Loh-Hagan

45th Parallel Press

Published in the United States of America by Cherry Lake Publishing
Ann Arbor, Michigan
www.cherrylakepublishing.com

Reading Adviser: Marla Conn MS, Ed., Literacy specialist, Read-Ability, Inc.
Book Designer: Felicia Macheske

Photo Credits: © Chris E. Heisey/Shutterstock.com, cover, 1; © Everett Historical/Shutterstock.com, 5; © Kristi Blokhin/Shutterstock.com, 6; © Tad Denson/Shutterstock.com, 11; © Evan McCaffrey/Shutterstock.com, 12, 18; Library of Congress, LC-DIG-ppmsca-33002, 17; Library of Congress, LC-DIG-ppmsca-33224, 21; Library of Congress, LC-DIG-pga-11166, 23; © George Sheldon/Shutterstock.com, 29

Graphic Elements Throughout: © Chipmunk131/Shutterstock.com; © Nowik Sylwia/Shutterstock.com; © Andrey_Popov/Shutterstock.com; © NadzeyaShanchuk/Shutterstock.com; © KathyGold/Shutterstock.com; © Black creator/Shutterstock.com; © Edvard Molnar/Shutterstock.com; © Elenadesign/Shutterstock.com; © estherpoon/Shutterstock.com

45th Parallel Press is an imprint of Cherry Lake Publishing.

Library of Congress Cataloging-in-Publication Data has been filed and is available at catalog.loc.gov

Cherry Lake Publishing would like to acknowledge the work of The Partnership for 21st Century Skills. Please visit www.p21.org for more information.

Printed in the United States of America
Corporate Graphics

A Note on Dramatic Retellings

Participating in Readers Theater, or dramatic retellings, can greatly improve reading skills, especially fluency. The books in the **BEHIND THE CURTAIN** series give readers opportunities to learn about important historical events in a fun and engaging way. These books serve as a bridge to more complex texts. All the characters are real figures from history; however, their stories have been fictionalized. To learn more about the people and the events, check out the Viewpoints and Perspectives series and the Perspectives Library series, as the **BEHIND THE CURTAIN** books are aligned to these stories.

TABLE of CONTENTS

HISTORICAL BACKGROUND

The U.S. Civil War was fought between the Northern and Southern states. It took place from 1861 to 1865. A major issue was slavery. The Northern states wanted to ban slavery. The Southern states wanted to keep it. The two sides disagreed. The South seceded from the United States.

Gettysburg is a city in Pennsylvania. The Battle of Gettysburg took place from July 1 to July 3, 1863. Confederate soldiers won a battle in Virginia. They felt good. They decided to invade the North. They fought against Union soldiers. General Robert E. Lee led the Confederates. General George G. Meade led the Union soldiers.

Vocabulary

slavery (SLAY-vur-ee) owning people as slaves

ban (BAN) to not allow

seceded (sih-SEED-id) left

Confederate (kuhn-FED-ur-it) the Southern slave states

Union (YOON-yuhn) the Northern free states

FLASH FACT!

Bodies covered the ground at Gettysburg.

Vocabulary

wounded (WOOND-id) hurt

captured (KAP-churd) taken prisoner

retreat (rih-TREET) to quit, to pull back

Lee wanted to destroy Union forces. He wanted to move the war out of the South. He wanted President Lincoln to stop the war. He wanted to get support from European countries. He wanted the South to be recognized as its own country. None of this happened.

The Battle of Gettysburg was the bloodiest battle in U.S. history. More people died than in any other battle. Between 46,000 and 51,000 people died. Many others were wounded. Many were captured. Many went missing. The South lost more men than the North.

The Battle of Gettysburg was a turning point in the war. The North won the battle. The South had to retreat. Many people lost faith in the South. The North eventually won the Civil War.

CAST of CHARACTERS

NARRATOR: person who helps tell the story

GEORGIA WADE MCCLELLAN: resident of the town of Gettysburg, mother of a young boy, sister of Ginnie Wade, Union supporter

ANNA PARKER: owner of a store in Gettysburg, wife of a Union soldier

GENERAL ROBERT E. LEE: main leader of the Confederate army, resident of Virginia

SAMUEL THORPE: Confederate soldier, resident of North Carolina

ALBERT SCHMIDT: Union soldier, member of the Iron **Brigade**, which is a group of soldiers from Wisconsin, Michigan, and Indiana

GENERAL ABNER DOUBLEDAY: leader of a group of Union soldiers

BACKSTORY
SPOTLIGHT BIOGRAPHY

Abraham Brian was a free black man. He bought a farm in 1857. He bought 12 acres (5 hectares). He grew wheat, barley, and hay. He also had apple and peach trees. His farm was just south of Gettysburg. Brian escaped right before the battle. He didn't want to be taken into slavery. He fled with his wife and children. Union troops took over his farm. They used his house as an office. They used his barn as a hospital. After the war, Brian returned to his farm. His house was destroyed. Its walls were filled with bullet holes. Its windows were broken. The fences were gone. The crops were trampled on. Dead soldiers were buried on his land. Brian asked for money to fix his house. He asked for $1,028. The government gave him $15. Brian rebuilt his farm. He sold it in 1869. He worked for a hotel. He died in 1875.

Vocabulary
resident (REZ-ih-duhnt)
a person who lives in a place
brigade (brih-GAYD)
a military group

FLASH FACT!
General George Meade commanded the Union troops at the Battle of Gettysburg.

ACT 1

NARRATOR: *It's June 30, 1863.* **GEORGIA WADE MCCLELLAN** *is in a shop owned by* **ANNA PARKER**.

GEORGIA: Have you heard from your husband?

ANNA: John is in Mississippi. He's fighting to keep the Union together.

GEORGIA: I can't believe the Southern states seceded. It's so **unpatriotic**. This war is nothing but bad news. Our men are risking their lives.

ANNA: Our lives have been affected too. Business has been hard. I can't get any **supplies**. I have to charge high prices. No one can pay.

GEORGIA: My sister, Ginnie, is staying with us now. Her husband was sent out to fight.

ANNA: My son and I saw some Confederate soldiers in our town.

GEORGIA: Oh no! What were they like? What did they want?

Vocabulary
unpatriotic (un-pay-tree-AH-tik)
not devoted to one's country
supplies (suh-PLYEZ)
materials needed to do something

FLASH FACT!
Some Confederate soldiers were in Gettysburg before the battle began.

ANNA: They wore rags. They didn't have shoes. They wanted supplies. But I didn't have anything to give them.

GEORGIA: The war has come to us. Yet all of our men are far away.

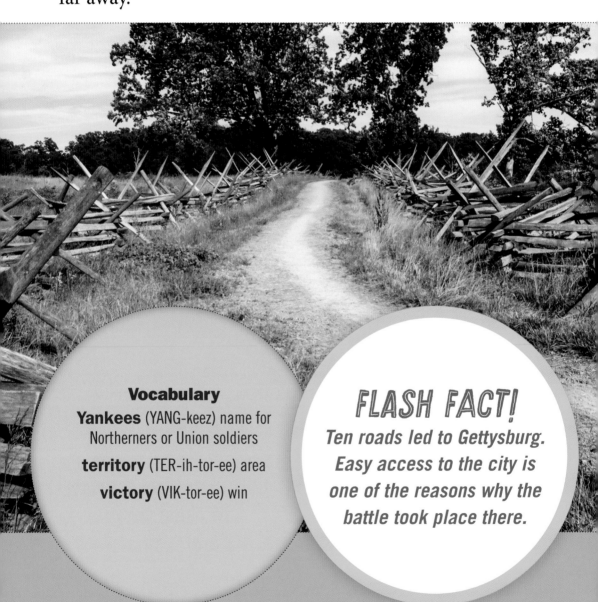

Vocabulary

Yankees (YANG-keez) name for Northerners or Union soldiers

territory (TER-ih-tor-ee) area

victory (VIK-tor-ee) win

FLASH FACT!

Ten roads led to Gettysburg. Easy access to the city is one of the reasons why the battle took place there.

NARRATOR: *It's July 1, 1863. Union and Confederate troops have marched to Gettysburg. They will soon meet.* **GENERAL ROBERT E. LEE** *and* **SAMUEL THORPE** *are talking.*

ROBERT: We need to beat the **Yankees** in their own **territory**.

SAMUEL: We beat them in the last battle. We have 75,000 strong troops. A **victory** should be easy.

ROBERT: The world needs to see us as a nation. When Britain and France see the North losing, they'll have to support us. This should end the Civil War. Lincoln will have to ask for peace.

SAMUEL: How can we lose? We're fighting for states' rights. Lincoln can't tell us what to do. We should be able to have slaves if we want.

NARRATOR: *It's a couple of hours later. The battle has begun.* **GENERAL ABNER DOUBLEDAY** *and* **ALBERT SCHMIDT** *are on the battlefield.*

ALBERT: I see the **rebels**! They're firing at us. They're pushing us back.

ABNER: Attack them back. Go into the woods. Push forward.

ALBERT: There's so much smoke. We're marching into a fire of bullets. I can't see. I can't hear. There's so many of them!

ABNER: That's what they're counting on. Lee thinks he'll beat us. He wants to destroy us now while we're **outnumbered**. But more Union troops are coming. Hold strong! Keep fighting. Dig **trenches**. Fight from inside them. Fire back. Get to the top of the hill. Act quick.

LOCATION SHOOTING
REAL-WORLD SETTING

Gettysburg National Cemetery is a special place. Union soldiers who died in the Battle of Gettysburg are buried there. The land was part of the battlefield. It was first called Soldiers' National Cemetery. There are 3,512 soldiers, including 979 unknown soldiers, buried there. There are also areas for soldiers who died in the Spanish–American War and World War I. Over 6,000 people are buried there. There's a monument in the cemetery. It's called the Soldiers' National Monument. It's 60 feet (18 meters) tall. It's made of granite. There's an iron fence called Sickles Fence. It separates Gettysburg National Cemetery from another cemetery. Daniel Sickles was a Union general. He fought at the Battle of Gettysburg. Before the war started, he shot Philip Barton Key. He thought Key was dating his wife.

Vocabulary

rebels (REB-uhlz) name for the Southern soldiers, people who resisted the government

outnumbered (out-NUHM-burd) one side having more numbers than the other; if you're outnumbered, you have fewer numbers

trenches (TRENCH-iz) long, narrow holes in the ground

FLASH FACT!
General Abner Doubleday and his wife were strong supporters of President Lincoln.

NARRATOR: *It's July 2, 1863. It's the second day of the battle.* **GENERAL ROBERT E. LEE** *and* **SAMUEL THORPE** *are talking at the Thompson House. This is Lee's headquarters. It's close to Gettysburg.*

SAMUEL: These Yankees are tougher than I thought. Victory doesn't seem so easy.

ROBERT: They've taken control of the hill. They're in a good spot. They can attack and defend. We need to fight harder. I had ordered troops to attack. We should have hit them from both the left and right sides. This needed to be done in the morning. What happened to my orders?

SAMUEL: There was a **delay**. We didn't attack until later in the afternoon. It was **brutal**. Our men fought for hours. The Union soldiers kept pushing forward. They gained some ground. But we beat them in the field.

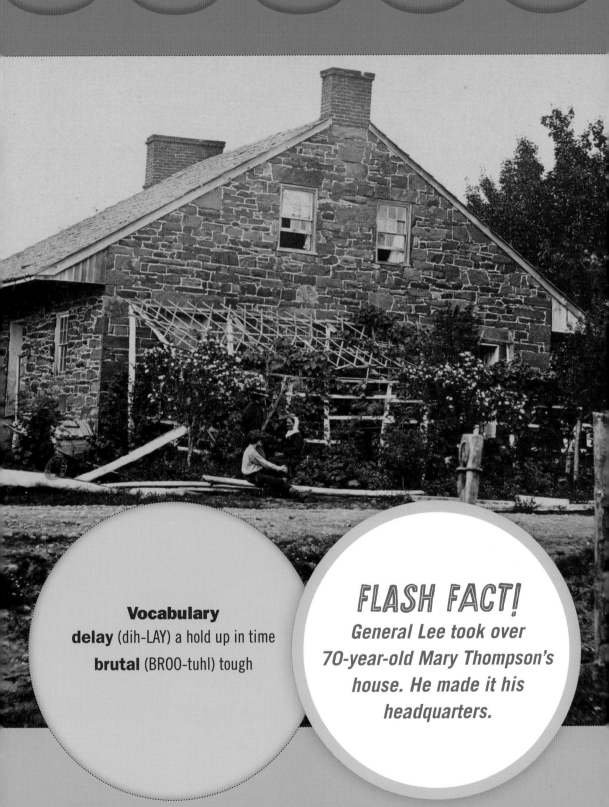

Vocabulary
delay (dih-LAY) a hold up in time
brutal (BROO-tuhl) tough

FLASH FACT!

General Lee took over 70-year-old Mary Thompson's house. He made it his headquarters.

ROBERT: How many men have we lost?

SAMUEL: There were so many bodies. We couldn't see the ground.

ROBERT: I don't want to lose any more men. But we must fight on.

NARRATOR: *It's the night of July 2, 1863.* **GEORGIA WADE MCCLELLAN** *is in* **ANNA PARKER'S** *shop.*

GEORGIA: Ginnie and I made food for our Union soldiers. They've been fighting for so long.

ANNA: I gave medical supplies to some hurt soldiers. The troops are using my shop as a hospital. But there's so much gunfire. I grabbed my children. We've been hiding in the **cellar**. Once, I came out to see what was happening. I saw Confederates chasing our soldiers.

GEORGIA: Our house is in the middle of everything. Bullets are hitting our roof and windows. But Ginnie wasn't scared. She continued to cook. The rest of us hid in the cellar. We only come out at night.

Vocabulary
cellar (SEL-ur) underground room

FLASH FACT!
Gettysburg residents could hear the noise from the battlefield.

ACT 2

NARRATOR: *It's July 3, 1863.* **GENERAL ABNER DOUBLEDAY** and **ALBERT SCHMIDT** *are at the top of the hill.*

ABNER: We can't lose again. Last night, the rebels got through our **defense**.

ALBERT: We still have the hill.

ABNER: How are our men?

ALBERT: They're tired of fighting.

ABNER: I'm tired too. But there's no time to rest. I hear gunfire again. The rebels are attacking. They're attacking our center.

ALBERT: We'll beat them back. They won't take this hill. We'll push them out.

ABNER: So many of our soldiers have died. We must remember all who gave their lives for the Union. We must fight for them!

Vocabulary
defense (dih-FENS)
line of protection

FLASH FACT!
The Gettysburg Gun is a cannon that was last used at the Battle of Gettysburg. It is now at the Rhode Island State House.

NARRATOR: GENERAL ROBERT E. LEE *and* **SAMUEL THORPE** *are at the battlefield.*

ROBERT: Let's end this battle. Let's end this war. Too many good people have died.

SAMUEL: What would you like to do?

ROBERT: Send in General Pickett and his men. Take our troops to the Union lines.

SAMUEL: Are you sure? We're not in the best **position** to fight the Yankees.

ROBERT: I'm giving the orders. Do as I say.

SAMUEL: Yes, sir.

Vocabulary
position (puh-ZISH-uhn) place

FLASH FACT!
Pickett's Charge was
named after General
George Pickett.

NARRATOR: *Several hours have passed.* **SAMUEL THORPE** *reports back to* **GENERAL ROBERT E. LEE**

SAMUEL: General Pickett charged. We fired. But it was hard fighting uphill. Plus more Union troops came. Pickett's men didn't stand a chance. There was too much gunfire. The Yankees made a wall of bullets.

ROBERT: How many men did we lose?

SAMUEL: We lost two-thirds of the men.

ROBERT: We also lost the battle. This is all my fault. I thought the Yankees were weakening. I thought they'd retreat. I was wrong.

Vocabulary
stained (STAYND) marked

wagon train (WAG-uhn) TRAYN) a line of wagons following each other

FLASH FACT!
After a rough start, the Union army won the Battle of Gettysburg.

SAMUEL: War is wrong.

ROBERT: This was a bloody loss. I will not lose any more men. Order our troops to retreat.

SAMUEL: It's raining.

ROBERT: Good.

SAMUEL: Why is rain good? It'll make it harder for us to move.

ROBERT: See those battlefields? They're **stained** with the blood of brave men. Maybe the rain will wash away the blood.

NARRATOR: *It's July 4, 1863. The battle is over.* **GENERAL ABNER DOUBLEDAY** *and* **ALBERT SCHMIDT** *are resting in town.*

ALBERT: The rebel troops are retreating. They're loading their wounded soldiers onto wagons. They're heading out of town. Their **wagon train** is 17 miles (27 kilometers) long.

ABNER: So many men died.

ALBERT: At least we won the battle!

ABNER: We won at great cost. This battle produced the most deaths ever.

ALBERT: I wish the South would stop fighting. I wish we could celebrate July 4th as one country.

NARRATOR: *It's July 5, 1863.* **GEORGIA WADE MCCLELLAN** *is in* **ANNA PARKER'S** *shop.*

ANNA: Why are you sad? There's no more fighting. The soldiers are almost gone. Now, we just need to bury the dead. We need to take care of the hurt soldiers. Things will get back to **normal** soon.

GEORGIA: Things will never be normal again. Ginnie is dead!

ANNA: Oh no! What happened?

GEORGIA: It happened on July 3rd. Ginnie went to get firewood. She wanted to bake more bread for the soldiers.

BLOOPERS
HISTORICAL MISTAKES

Many experts think Pickett's Charge was one of the worst military mistakes ever. Pickett's Charge was named after General George Pickett. He was one of General Robert E. Lee's soldiers. Pickett's Charge took place on July 3, 1863. It marked the end of the Battle of Gettysburg. It was the last time Lee invaded the North. Military experts say Lee should've marched to Philadelphia. Instead, Lee marched to Gettysburg. This was a bad move. Lee ordered Pickett's troops to charge. His troops marched right into the Union's guns and cannons. Half of the soldiers died. Pickett's soldiers had to walk across 1 mile (1.6 km) of open ground. This made them easy targets. Pickett was blamed for the loss. But he was just following Lee's orders. Lee said many times, "The blame is mine."

Vocabulary
normal (NOR-muhl)
usual, typical, expected

FLASH FACT!
More officers were killed at Gettysburg than in any other Civil War battle.

ANNA: Ginnie is such a caring person.

GEORGIA: Confederate bullets hit the house. One hit my bed. Another bullet went through two closed doors. It hit Ginnie in the back. It hit her heart. Ginnie was standing in the kitchen. She fell to the floor. She was dead before I even got to her!

ANNA: Oh dear! She was only 20 years old.

GEORGIA: I yelled. I cried. Union soldiers heard me. They came in. They took me down to our cellar. They didn't want me to get hit.

ANNA: What happened to Ginnie's body?

GEORGIA: I wrapped her in our family **quilt**. I buried her in our backyard. I'll move her body to a **cemetery** later.

ANNA: Ginnie is the only **civilian** killed in this battle.

GEORGIA: I wish no one was killed.

Vocabulary

quilt (KWILT) blanket

cemetery (SEM-ih-ter-ee) a place where dead bodies are buried

civilian (suh-VIL-yuhn) a person who is not in the military

FLASH FACT!

Newspaper reporters incorrectly spelled Ginnie's name "Jennie." There's a statue of her where she's buried.

EVENT TIMELINE

May 9, 1820: The Missouri Compromise is passed. This allows Missouri to enter the United States as a slave slate. Maine enters as a free state. Several laws are passed about this issue. Some states come in as slave states. Some come in as free states. Slave states allow slavery. Free states do not.

September 18, 1850: The Fugitive Slave Act is passed. The United States bans efforts to stop the capture of runaway slaves. Slavery is a major issue. It divides the North and South.

November 6, 1860: Abraham Lincoln is elected the U.S. president. None of the slave states support him. Eleven Southern states leave the Union.

April 12, 1861: The Confederates attack Fort Sumter. The Civil War begins.

January 1, 1863: President Lincoln signs the Emancipation Proclamation. This frees all slaves in the Southern states.

June 30, 1863: The Confederates spot Union troops heading toward Gettysburg.

July 1, 1863: The battle begins. Soldiers from both sides reach Gettysburg. They fight. There's a total of 90,000 soldiers. The fighting continues until nightfall.

July 2, 1863: Confederate troops are ordered to attack Union troops. One of the Confederate troops is delayed. This gives Union troops time to strengthen their forts.

July 3, 1863: Union troops fire cannons. They force the Confederate troops down the hill. General George Pickett orders 15,000 Confederate troops to attack. Union troops fire. The Confederates retreat. They lose. The battle is over.

July 4, 1863: The Confederate army returns to Virginia.

November 19, 1863: A section of the Gettysburg battlefield becomes a cemetery. Union soldiers are buried there. Lincoln gives the Gettysburg Address.

April 9, 1865: General Lee surrenders. He does this at Appomattox Courthouse in Virginia. The Union wins the war.

December 18, 1865: The 13th Amendment to the U.S. Constitution passes. It bans slavery.

CONSIDER THIS!

TAKE A POSITION! Learn more about General Robert E. Lee. Lee believed more in the Northern states' ideas. But he felt it was his duty to defend Virginia. Lincoln wanted Lee to lead his armies. But Lee said no. He fought for the South. Did Lee make the right decision? What were his reasons? Do you agree or disagree with him? Argue your point with reasons and evidence.

SAY WHAT? The Battle of Gettysburg is known as a turning point for the U.S. Civil War. Explain what this means. Explain why the Battle of Gettysburg was important.

THINK ABOUT IT! Study Lincoln's Gettysburg Address. This is a famous speech. What does it mean? Why is it important? If you were President Lincoln, what would you say?

LEARN MORE

Baxter, Roberta. *The Battle of Gettysburg*. Ann Arbor, MI: Cherry Lake Publishing, 2014.

Martin, Iain C. Gettysburg: *The True Account of Two Young Heroes in the Greatest Battle of the Civil War*. New York: Sky Pony Press, 2013.

O'Connor, Jim. *What Was the Battle of Gettysburg?* New York: Grosset and Dunlap, 2013.

Russo, Kristin J. *Viewpoints on the Battle of Gettysburg*. Ann Arbor, MI: Cherry Lake Publishing, 2018.

INDEX

ABOUT THE AUTHOR

Dr. Virginia Loh-Hagan is an author, university professor, and former classroom teacher. When she was in elementary school, she was in a school play. She memorized Lincoln's Gettysburg Address. Unfortunately, she got old. So, she doesn't remember it anymore. She lives in San Diego with her very tall husband and very naughty dogs. To learn more about her, visit www.virginialoh.com.